Car Stars
MASERATI
GRANTURISMO

by Julie Murray

Dash!
LEVELED READERS
An Imprint of Abdo Zoom • abdobooks.com

Dash!
LEVELED READERS

Level 1 – Beginning
Short and simple sentences with familiar words or patterns for children who are beginning to understand how letters and sounds go together.

Level 2 – Emerging
Longer words and sentences with more complex language patterns for readers who are practicing common words and letter sounds.

Level 3 – Transitional
More developed language and vocabulary for readers who are becoming more independent.

THIS BOOK CONTAINS
RECYCLED MATERIALS

abdobooks.com

Published by Abdo Zoom, a division of ABDO, PO Box 398166, Minneapolis, Minnesota 55439.
Copyright © 2020 by Abdo Consulting Group, Inc. International copyrights reserved in all countries.
No part of this book may be reproduced in any form without written permission from the publisher.
Dash!™ is a trademark and logo of Abdo Zoom.

Printed in the United States of America, North Mankato, Minnesota.
102019
012020

Photo Credits: Alamy, Getty Images, iStock, Shutterstock, ©The Car Spy p.10 / CC BY 2.0
Production Contributors: Kenny Abdo, Jennie Forsberg, Grace Hansen, John Hansen
Design Contributors: Dorothy Toth, Neil Klinepier

Library of Congress Control Number: 2019941268

Publisher's Cataloging in Publication Data

Names: Murray, Julie, author.
Title: Maserati GranTurismo / by Julie Murray
Description: Minneapolis, Minnesota : Abdo Zoom, 2020 | Series: Car stars | Includes online resources and index.
Identifiers: ISBN 9781532129155 (lib. bdg.) | ISBN 9781098220136 (ebook) | ISBN 9781098220624 (Read-to-Me ebook)
Subjects: LCSH: Maserati GranTurismo automobile--Juvenile literature. | Cars (Automobiles)--Juvenile literature. | Sports cars--Juvenile literature. | Vehicles--Juvenile literature.
Classification: DDC 629.2222--dc23

Table of Contents

Maserati GranTurismo

The GranTurismo (GT) is an Italian **sports car.**

The first GT came out in 2007.
It was fast and lightweight.

The 2019 MC **model** can go from 0 to 60 mph (0-96.5 kph) in 4.7 seconds. Its top speed is 187 mph (301 kph).

The GT has a 4.7-liter **V8** engine. It has 454 **HP**.

The Look

The GT is a two-door car.
It has 2+2 seating.

The GT sits low to the ground. It has a large front grill. Three air vents are on each side.

The inside has hand-stitched leather seats. It has an 8.4-inch (21.3 cm) touchscreen. This controls air, audio, and navigation.

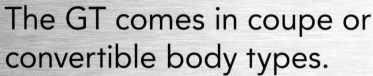

The GT comes in coupe or convertible body types.

It is an **expensive** car. Prices for the 2019 GT Sport start at around $150,000.

More Facts

- The MC Stradale is a two-seater. It is the only Maserati GT to have this feature.

- Production of the Maserati GT is set to end in 2019.

- The trident is the symbol of Maserati. It is a three-pronged spear.

Glossary

expensive – costing a lot of money.

HP – short for horsepower. A unit of energy equal to 746 watts of the energy needed to lift 550 pounds in one second, used in measuring the power of engines.

model – a particular type or style of product.

sports car – a low-built car designed for performance at high speeds.

V8 – an engine with 8 cylinders mounted on the crankcase in two sets of four.

Index

Online Resources

Booklinks
NONFICTION NETWORK
FREE! ONLINE NONFICTION RESOURCES

To learn more about the Maserati GranTurismo, please visit **abdobooklinks.com** or scan this QR code. These links are routinely monitored and updated to provide the most current information available.